MINDSET

Lela Haase

"Scripture quotations are from The ESV® Bible (The Holy Bible, English Standard Version®), copyright © 2001 by Crossway, a publishing ministry of Good News Publishers. Used by permission. All rights reserved."

Scripture quotations marked TPT are from The Passion Translation®. Copyright © 2017, 2018, 2020 by Passion & Fire Ministries, Inc. Used by permission. All rights reserved. ThePassionTranslation.com.

"Scripture quotations taken from the Amplified® Bible (AMPC), Copyright © 1954, 1958, 1962, 1964, 1965, 1987 by The Lockman Foundation. Used by permission. www.lockman.org"

First Printing 2025

ISBN 978-1-7378124-4-9
Copyright © 2025 Treign Publishing. All rights reserved.
Printed in the USA.

Contents

Introduction: The Importance of the Word

Chapter 1   The Mind is Where We Deal With Life
Chapter 2   Spirit, Soul, and Body
Chapter 3   God Equipped Us to Overcome
Chapter 4   What Are You Meditating On
Chapter 5   How to Control Our Thoughts
Chapter 6   Pay Attention to Your Emotions
Chapter 7   Take Captive Your Mind
Chapter 8   Bringing Our Thoughts Into the Obedience of Christ
Chapter 9   Dismantle the Wrong Thoughts
Chapter 10 Fortify Our Mind

Mindset

Introduction

Because of the importance of the Word of God and its power to transform our lives, it is important to have a study aid in studying topics. This mini book was created to help you continue studying and growing in your personal walk with God. This will be a practical reference to help you meditate on the Word.

The mini book focuses on the mind, which is the battleground for our souls. It is here we have to equip ourselves to fight thoughts from the enemy that cause us to have wrong thinking. This mini book contains guidelines to help you take captive your thought life and live the life God wants for you.

May you be blessed as you read and study this mini book.

Chapter 1

The Mind is Where We Deal with Life

It is where we process life.

It is essential to understand how the mind works so that we can be guided by the Spirit of God and live a life of victory, as God intended for us to do.

What is in our mind influences the decisions we make.

Our mind is our soul, and it is composed of our mind, will, and emotions.

Our thoughts activate emotions, which in turn influence our will and the decisions we make.

- It is like a domino effect.

- The mind, will, and emotions work together as a team.

To achieve victory over our mind, will, and emotions, we must understand our soul and how it functions.

So this is why we abandon everything morally impure and all forms of wicked conduct. Instead, with a sensitive spirit we absorb God's Word, which has been implanted within our nature, for the Word of Life has power to continually deliver us.

James 1:21 TPT

Based on this scripture, there is only one way to overcome our mind, will, and emotions, and that is to absorb the Word of God. That is it. **There is no other way.**

- The Word must be implanted.

- How we deal with our thoughts and feelings affects the events of our lives.
- It affects how we **live** our lives.
- It could be said that our mind activity becomes our physical reality.

When I think of the word absorb, I think of a sponge. A sponge soaks up all the water. It incorporates that liquid into its spongy surface and that liquid becomes part of that sponge. That liquid occupies and fills the sponge.

Notes

Chapter 2

Our Mind is Our Soul

Now, may the God of peace and harmony set you apart, making you completely holy. And may your entire being—spirit, soul, and body—be kept completely flawless in the appearing of our Lord Jesus, the Anointed One.

I Thessalonians 5:23 TPT

We have often heard the term "soul" when talking about people coming to the Lord. But the soul is not our spirit. Our spirit is where we are born again and commune with Jesus. They are different things.

This verse reveals that we are composed of three distinct parts which are spirit, soul, and body.

The goal is for the spirit, soul, and body to work together, being controlled by the spirit. However, that is not automatic and requires us to allow this to happen by renewing our minds and learning to control our flesh by dying to ourselves.

Stop imitating the ideals and opinions of the culture around you but be inwardly transformed by the Holy Spirit through a total reformation of how you think. This will empower you to discern God's will as you live a beautiful life, satisfying and perfect in his eyes.

Romans 12:2 TPT

It is essential to learn how to quiet our minds so that we can effectively control it.

The mind can be so loud that we miss the voice of the Spirit of God.

This scripture is saying that there are things around us that are not truth, and we therefore need to do a mental reboot to think according to the Word.

Notes

Chapter 3

<u>God Equipped Us to Overcome</u>

We can change our thoughts when we renew our minds. Our minds and thoughts do not have to control us.

For though we walk (live) in the flesh, we are not carrying on our warfare according to the flesh and using mere human weapons.

For the weapons of our warfare are not physical [weapons of flesh and blood], but they are mighty before God for the overthrow and destruction of strongholds,

[Inasmuch as we] refute arguments and theories and reasonings and every proud and lofty thing that sets itself up against the [true] knowledge of God; and we lead every

thought and *purpose away captive into the obedience of Christ (the Messiah, the Anointed One)*

II Corinthians 10:3-5 AMPC

It makes me sad to see believers oppressed and controlled by their thoughts and feelings.

- This happens because believers do not know how to deal with their thoughts, and they let them run wild in their head.

Believers can struggle with particular mindsets, ideas, or thoughts that are not grounded in Scripture.

- We operate from how our minds are set.
- What we think about grows in us.
- Our thoughts shape who we are.

Notice verse five in the previous passage. It says **we refute arguments.**

This passage refers to our mind. Therefore, we refute the argument that suggests it is not in line with the Word of God.

- This passage also says that we bring or lead the wrong thought to the truth.
- We hold it captive, meaning it can only think one way, and that is the way of the Word. The way of truth.
- When we notice those thoughts, we speak to them and then speak to the Word to bring them into the captivity of the truth. Essentially, they are not allowed to do as they please, but only as the Word permits them to do.

Notes

Chapter 4

What are You Meditating on?

Meditation is a word that Satan has negatively attacked. Meditation first came from God before Satan perverted it. It simply means to think about or consider something. Essentially, it involves repeatedly turning something over in your mind. This is my definition of the word.

We can ponder on Scriptures. We can spend a considerable amount of time thinking about them, dissecting them, and examining them thoroughly. That is Biblical meditation in its simplest form.

Compare Biblical meditation to rehearsing for a play. A group at my church puts on a play each year to raise money for missions. They rehearse their lines over and over, practicing the play so often that when the day of the event arrives, they are ready because they have thoroughly rehearsed. This is how it is with Biblical meditation.

So, back to the question. What are you meditating on? What do you play over and over in your mind?

- What we meditate on and think on shapes our actions.
- If our thoughts are bad, our actions are bad.
- If our thoughts are good, our actions are good.

Here is an example. If you think you're a loser, then you start feeling like a loser, which in turn affects your decisions, choices, and ultimately how you feel about yourself, because you have adopted the loser mindset.

All this came from your mindset about yourself. If you rehearse over and over what a loser you are, that is what you will become.

It is vitally important that we meditate on the truth of God's Word. That is what will set us free, and that will be what affects our decisions, our choices, and ultimately how we live our lives and feel about ourselves.

If we think we are an overcomer, we start feeling like an overcomer, which in turn affects our decision, choices, and ultimately how we feel about ourselves, because we have adopted the overcomer mindset.

Notes

Chapter 5

How to Control Our Thoughts

God wants us to know how to control our thoughts so that they don't control us. Our thoughts shape us, even if we don't like that. God wants us to be kingdom minded and shaped for our purpose on this earth.

For the weapons of our warfare are not of the flesh but have divine power to destroy strongholds.

II Corinthians 10:4 ESV

Notice the word "warfare" in the previous passage.

Warfare is a well-planned attack.

- This means we are in a war.
- The devil has a well-planned attack to get us in the wrong mindset so he can have access to our lives.
- Notice – God has a plan. That plan was already completed at Calvary, and now we are to operate in it.
- The Holy Spirit has given us a strategy to overcome and control our thoughts.

Inasmuch as we refute arguments and theories and reasonings and every proud and lofty thing that sets itself up against the [true] knowledge of God; and we lead every thought and purpose away captive into the obedience of Christ (the Messiah, the Anointed One)

II Corinthians 10:5 AMPC

- We have thoughts.
- We have a thought pattern.
- These thought patterns were built over a lifetime.

Patterns form in the following ways.

- A thought comes to us (It is a lie from the enemy. It might be something like you are a failure.)
- Life seems to have reinforced this lie.
- People may do things or say things that cause you to believe the lie.
- Situations may happen that cause you to believe the lie.

Sadly, people can significantly impact us through their words and actions. We must learn not to be moved by these things, but to be moved only by the Word and what It says about us.

Notes

Chapter 6

Pay Attention to Your Emotions

If you notice that your emotions and feelings are taking control, ask yourself why you are feeling this way. Pay attention to what you are thinking and learn to recognize how you feel.

The question to ask yourself when you're having emotions all over the place is, what have I been thinking about?

Remember that feelings are part of the soul, and therefore, what is going on in your mind will create certain emotions.

At one point in my life, I struggled with feeling like God could never use me again. A friend had betrayed me, just as Judas betrayed Jesus. I struggled for a long time with feelings of condemnation. He forgave me, I knew, but He could not use me. Of course, this was a lie from the devil.

One day, I questioned the Lord aloud, "Why am I feeling this way? It's not very nice, and I don't want to feel this way anymore." I heard the word "perfect" come up in my spirit. I began to meditate on that, and suddenly, a surge of power filled me. I started to declare that I am perfect! There is no one more perfect than I am.

See, my natural self is not perfect. I make many mistakes, but my spirit, where God lives, is perfect, and my spirit is the real me, not this natural self.

Immediately, my feelings changed because my thoughts changed.

Why did I talk to myself out loud?

- You cannot simply think yourself out of wrong thoughts.
- You must do something.
- God does not magically take away your wrong thoughts.
- **You** renew your mind.
- We are in a war, and war requires action.
- Faith comes by hearing. We need to hear the truth. It gives us power.
- We are resetting or reprogramming our minds to think correctly.
- If we do not reset our thoughts, the thoughts will reset us according to their image.

This is why we must speak and command our minds to align with the Word.

Notes

Chapter 7

The Little Rebel

Our minds want to be what I call "little rebels." Your mind likes to do what it wants, when it wants, and think according to the flesh.

Your mind is like a child. A child likes to run and grab the ball off the road. They are only thinking about getting the ball back. An adult provides direction to a child for their own safety. The child does not realize the danger of the street where the ball has gone.

This is our mind. It must be directed to obey God's things. It wants to play in the street and do the things that are harmful to our choices and emotions. These things can even torment us because they do not line up with the Word of God.

Stop imitating the ideals and opinions of the culture around you but be inwardly transformed by the Holy Spirit through a total reformation of how you think. This will empower you to discern God's will as you live a beautiful life, satisfying and perfect in his eyes.

Romans 12:2 TPT

[Inasmuch as we] refute arguments and theories and reasonings and every proud and lofty thing that sets itself up against the [true] knowledge of God; and we lead every thought and purpose away captive into the obedience of Christ (the Messiah, the Anointed One)

II Corinthians 10:5 AMPC

When I think of the word "captive", I think of someone who has been arrested. What happens when someone is arrested? They are imprisoned, caged, or confined. How does this relate to your thoughts?

When a thought comes, we confine it. The cage it is confined in is the Word of God. We hold those thoughts in the cage of the Word, what God's laws are, and what our rights are in Him.

Here are some thoughts to cage.

- I am chosen.
- I am forgiven.
- I am a child of God.
- I am set free.
- I am PERFECT.

The real us is perfect. Our natural man is not perfect. That is a truth we must think on and embrace.

I take every thought and cage it in the cage of the Word.

Chapter 8

Thoughts are to Obey

Our thoughts are to come into the obedience of Christ. Here is an example of what that means.

A child will obey. They can obey the easy way. The easiest way is for the parent to say it and the child to do it. Then there is the hard way. The parents say it, and the child protests, throwing a fit. Either way, the child will obey. If we are Godly parents, we will ensure that our children obey. The hard way means that the parent may have to punish the child so that what is said can be done.

There you have it, the easy way or the hard way. This is precisely what we do with our thoughts. We take those little rebels" and force them to obey the truth of God's Word. The mind, will, and emotions will not like this at first, just like a child who does not want to obey. Your feelings may rebel and kick into full gear.

- We must speak to our mind, will, and emotions, and tell them they are going to do it, period. It can be done the easy way or the hard way. But they will obey, and these feelings will not control us.
- We have to die to our feelings and our flesh. This is the most painful process we can experience.

Obedience means subdue. When we subdue something, it is brought into obedience by force. We have to set the standard that we will not allow our soul to rule us. It will obey what God says.

Obedience also means pulling down.

- We are dismantling the lie at the root.
- We are breaking those wrong thoughts apart.

Remember my testimony earlier? I dismantled the lie of being a failure and never being used by God again simply by speaking to those wrong thoughts and telling them that I am perfect. The real me, my spirit, is perfect.

In essence, I made my wrong thought captive to the truth of God's Word. My thoughts had to conform, and joy came into my life.

Notes

Chapter 9

<u>Dismantle Wrong Thoughts</u>

Why is it important to dismantle the wrong thoughts?

The longer we think incorrectly and not according to the Word, the stronger the wrong thoughts become in us.

Stronger makes something become a stronghold.

- A stronghold is simply something that has a strong hold on us.
- It is layer upon layer of thoughts. The thought layers can be good or bad.
- It is like a fortified wall.

Whatever has that strong hold on us and has been layered on us is what creates our mindset.

The longer we think correctly and in accordance with the Word, the stronger the Word becomes within us.

Often, strongholds become so ingrained in us that we don't realize they are even there.

What has a strong or powerful hold in your life?

- Meditating on the wrong things will build a stronghold in your life from the devil.
- Meditating on the Word of God will build a stronghold against the schemes of the devil.
- What are you meditating on?

How would you react if someone came up behind you and put a strong or powerful hold on you? If someone put their arms around you and held you firmly so you could not move, you would fight that person. You would fight for your freedom. That is exactly what we must do with the mindsets that are wrong and have taken a strong or powerful hold on us.

Notes

Chapter 10

Fortified Minds

We want our minds to be fortified. We fortify the mind with the Word of God. When something is fortified, the weapon cannot penetrate it. When your mind is fortified, the lies of the devil may come for a moment, but they cannot set up camp and make a stronghold because we have learned to notice the lie more quickly now.

For the weapons of our warfare are not physical [weapons of flesh and blood], but they are mighty before God for the overthrow and destruction of strongholds,

II Corinthians 10:4 AMPC

I love that our weapons are mighty! They are not anything natural. We combat with the Word. The word mighty means it has explosive power! We have the explosive power to put the devil on the run and take control of our minds!

It is only through God that we have victory. It can be done in no other way. It is through the mighty, explosive power of God that we set the enemy running. The Word of God applied in our lives is the only way it can be done.

We are literally infused with the mighty power of God! We are victorious!

For the rest, brethren, whatever is true, whatever is worthy of reverence and is honorable and seemly, whatever is just, whatever is pure, whatever is lovely and lovable, whatever is kind and winsome and gracious, if there is any virtue and excellence, if there is anything worthy of praise, think on and weigh and take account of these things [fix your minds on them].

Philippians 4:8 AMPC

Paul was in prison when he wrote the letter to the church in Philippi. Yet, he was refusing to allow the thoughts of the devil to dominate his life. He was thinking of the goodness of God.

This is how we take our minds captive and walk in the mindset of the Kingdom of God. We fix our minds on the truth only. When we recognize evil thoughts, we cast them down and eliminate them, replacing them with God thoughts.

What does God's Word say about you? God's Word cannot lie.

- You reign in life.
- You are chosen.

- You are perfect.
- You are justified.
- You are forgiven.
- You are heirs and co-heirs with Christ.
- You are seated with Christ.
- You are crowned.
- You are redeemed.
- You are set free.
- You are not forsaken.
- You are more than a conqueror.
- You are victorious.
- You are undefeated.
- You are a winner.

There are many more things to add to this list. I encourage you to find those things in the Word and begin to think about them.

Prayer of Salvation

If you do not know Jesus as your Lord and Savior, I would like to take a moment to guide you through the prayer of salvation.

Dear Heavenly Father,
Please forgive me for my sins. I believe you died and rose again for my salvation. Your blood sets me free, and I accept you now as my Lord and Savior.
In Jesus' Mighty Name,
Amen

If you are going to grow as a believer it is vital that you read your Bible, pray every day, and find a local church to attend in person every Sunday. This will help you to walk out your new life in Christ.

The old has passed away, and now everything is new.
Welcome to the family!

Lela Haase is an international Bible teacher who has dedicated her life to growing the leaders and ministers in the Body of Christ around the world. She and her family spent ten years in the Philippines and now travel the world sharing the Good News of the Gospel with ministers and leaders. Lela, she along with her husband, Bob, are the founders of Step of Faith Ministries International Inc. in 1996 and is currently building a missionary training center in Catanauan, Quezon, Philippines.

Step of Faith Ministries Intl
P.O. Box 972
Mannford, OK. 74044
918-361-8547

stepoffaithint.com

Step of Faith Ministries Intl

Step of Faith Ministries International